String Art

SYMMOGRAPHY

Three-Dimensional Creative
Designs with Yarn
without Knotting or Knitting

by Lois Kreischer

Crown Publishers, Inc.   New York

This book was originally published as *Symmography*.

ISBN: 0-517-502747
ISBN: 0-517-N04901
Fourth Printing, February, 1973

Contents

Introduction

Symmography is an art form using yarn, wood, and nails as the media. It has evolved through a process of experimentation. My start was with very simple but quite mathematically precise designs and later I began to tackle more difficult feats such as the Golden Gate Bridge. I thus found that a fairly elementary art form could be developed into a mature and sophisticated medium of expression.

The word symmography is derived from "symmetry" and the suffix "-graphy." Together they describe a linear representation in which proportion, balance, and harmony are used to create the proper relationship of rays of yarn to one another, thus producing an aesthetically pleasing picture.

I have written this book in the first person. This is somewhat unconventional for an instructional book, but I feel strongly that I am not imparting the way to create symmographs, but rather sharing my experiences and processes as explicitly as possible as a stepping-off point so others may also find enjoyment and fulfillment through symmography. So, have fun and come join me in my experiment.

Materials Needed

The materials you need to begin a symmograph are basically quite simple and inexpensive, many of which you already have around the home. The musts are: nails, hammer, piece of wood, and yarn. I will go into these and other "nice to haves" in greater detail so that I can share the results of what I have found "works" after a great deal of experimentation.

Nails: The nails I use for my symmographic creations are fairly narrow "bright steel wire," with small heads which are necessary to keep the yarn from sliding off the tops of the nails. I prefer 1" or 7/8" nails. I have found that 1-1/4" nails are a bit long and somewhat difficult to pound in straight, but I also admit to being a novice carpenter. The 3/4" nails are adequate, but are a little short for some pictures in which the nails must carry many layers of yarn. The 1" nails seem to be ideal for me, but any length that suits your purpose and is successfully handled is fine. Experimentation with various

Materials needed

lengths as well as things like furniture tacks, linoleum tacks, cup hooks, tacks—plain or colored—is highly recommended and produces various interesting effects.

Wood: It is fun to use various shapes and sizes of wood as backgrounds for symmographic pictures. In fact, I have found that a picture is often inspired by the shape or size or grain of a certain piece of wood. As to the thickness of the wood, I have found that 1/2" works best; 1/4" tends to warp; 3/8" is adequate but the nails frequently go clear through; 5/8" or thicker gets heavy for hanging and is difficult to frame, if so desired.

So far, I have been using indoor plywood. It is inexpensive and easily obtainable. I began by buying precut pieces from a cabinetmaking lumberyard. I was able to get interesting sizes and had the opportunity to be very choosy as to placement of knots, if any, and the pieces were very well cut. I have, however, also bought the wood by the 4' × 8' sheet and had it cut. To save on cutting fees, I have it cut into three or four pieces and finish cutting it down myself to desired size. However, I recommend the professional cut if you can afford it and know the sizes you want.

Plywood is the least expensive, but the other woods handle beautifully. The nicer grains, without the problem of working around knotholes, might be worth the higher price.

Yarns: I have had success using four-ply wool knitting worsted and Orlon acrylic. They seem to be the least expensive and come in a wide variety of colors. People have often registered surprise since the yarn looks narrower when seen on a picture, but that is because it is quite tightly stretched between nails. Other size yarns offer possibilities for various effects. As an example, I used some mohair yarn in the Peacock shown here in order to obtain the feathery effect of the ostentatious tail.

Tools: A **Hammer** is a necessity. **Pliers, Scissors, Masking Tape, Tweezers, Sandpaper,** and **Yarn Needle** (I like a plastic yarn needle for weaving in ends and a large-eyed darning needle or metal yarn needle for going through holes in the wood) are all useful and good to have on hand.

Stain: I prefer a dark walnut stain for backgrounds but you could use many others.

Paints: For backgrounds as well as frames I like acrylics, since they are fast drying and make brush cleaning easy.

Brushes: You will need paintbrushes for painting and staining.

Peacock. Use of mohair yarn in tail

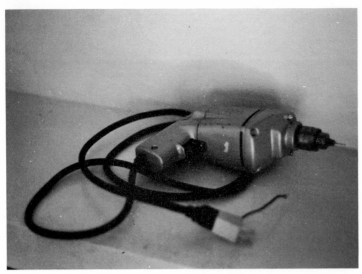

Electric drill

Pencils, Eraser, Ruler, Compass, Protractor, and **T-Square** can all be put to good use when drawing the pattern for the picture.

Paper: I use shelf paper for drawing my pictures initially. I keep both the 13" and the 18" rolls on hand since sometimes one and sometimes the other is closer to the appropriate size.

Glue: This is used for gluing paper to obtain the size of the picture as well as for gluing frame corners. A white, clear drying glue is best.

Drill: The only fairly expensive tool for the symmograph itself which is "nice to have" is an electric drill. I prefer the variable speed, and I use a 1/16" bit or smaller for transferring patterns and a 1/8" if I want holes through which to thread yarn.

Ideas

I am not sure at exactly what point an idea for a symmograph comes to me. Sometimes it is fully conceived before I begin any preparations for a picture. Sometimes it is inspired by wood of a certain shape. Sometimes it comes from wanting to try a different color as a background or to experiment with a new combination of yarn colors or to achieve a different effect.

Sometimes even the grain of a certain piece of wood inspires me. That is to say, the preparation of wood can and often does precede the formulation of the idea, but since the idea more frequently comes first, I will deal with them in that order.

I have found through my experience in symmography that a simple idea is more successful than a very complicated one. By "simple" I mean one without a great deal of detail since the weaving patterns of the yarns make the picture quite intricate and decorative. I have also found more success when striving for a decorative effect rather than for strict realism.

You might also keep in mind that the more complex a design is, the larger it will have to be. The reverse of this is the fact that if you want a small picture, the design will need to be extremely simple.

A list of possible ideas might include animals, insects, birds, objects, free-flowing designs or abstracts, geometrical shapes, faces, structures, and many others.

Preparing the Wood

The first step in preparing the wood for a symmograph is either to cut the wood to a size that will most enhance your design or choose the board from precut pieces that is most appropriate. Then sand edges and surface, if needed, to ensure

Octo. Painted background

smooth handling and to clean sufficiently. If staining the wood, apply one or more coats until the desired color is obtained. For those who have never stained wood before, explicit directions can be found on the can of stain.

If a painted background is desired, as in the case of Octo pictured here, apply as many coats of acrylic paint as necessary to obtain the color you want. I find two coats usually necessary. Allow to dry thoroughly.

Using a spray paint is another possibility for obtaining a painted background, but I have not found it nearly as effective as the acrylics.

Drawing the Pattern

One of the most mystifying aspects of my creations to the observer, and probably the most frequently asked question is: "How do you know where to put the nails?" The answer is simply that I draw my picture on paper first and use it as a pattern.

I begin by cutting a piece of shelf paper or gluing pieces together if necessary to get a piece exactly the size of the wood I will use as a background. I then mark off a 1-1/2" to 2" margin or border around all the edges (narrower if making a small picture) to enable me to fill up my available space and as a guide to leave sufficient room for the frame. Since many of my symmographs involve balance and symmetry, I also mark the horizontal and vertical centers of the picture to use as points of reference.

This is followed by the actual drawing of the picture or design. If it is a symmetrical picture, I draw one side, then trace it over to the other half. I do this by drawing it very dark so it can be traced through to the back, then with the paper folded, it can be seen through on the other side and thus traced. Precision is necessary if the design is geometrical and/or symmetrical. I find that large and simple designs work best since the weave of the yarns is so decorative.

Once the design has been drawn to my satisfaction, it is time to mark off the placement of nails. For curved lines, intervals of 1/2", 3/4", or 1" work well. This depends upon the size of the design (in a small design, nails may need to be even closer together than 1/2" to obtain desired effect) and the smoothness of the curve desired (the closer the nails, the smoother the curve—see Diagram 1). If straight lines are called for, nail markings should be placed as needed.

Diagram 1. Close nails give a smooth curve

Nail markings can be measured off with a ruler, compass, protractor, T-square, or whatever best suits the need of the line. Many times I rely on my own judgment as to where the nail markings should go. If a symmetrical design is being created, it is probably worthwhile to transfer markings for nails from one side to the other to assure balance and correct placement. This can be done easily by folding the picture in half and placing it on a newspaper or magazine with the already marked side up, then puncturing both sides with a pin or needle at marked intervals.

The following are examples of patterns that have been drawn and marked for nail placement. The Butterfly exemplifies the symmetrical design.

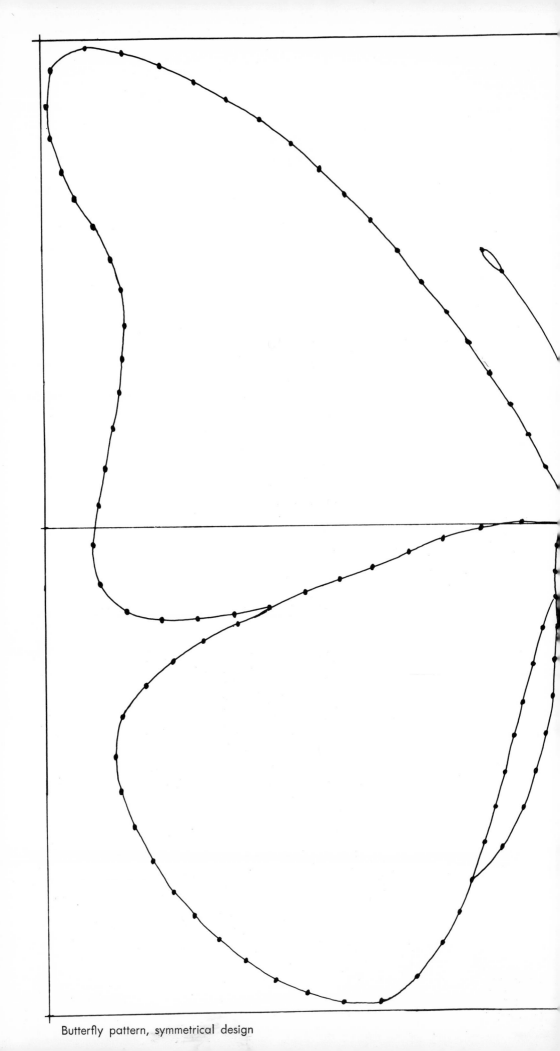

Butterfly pattern, symmetrical design

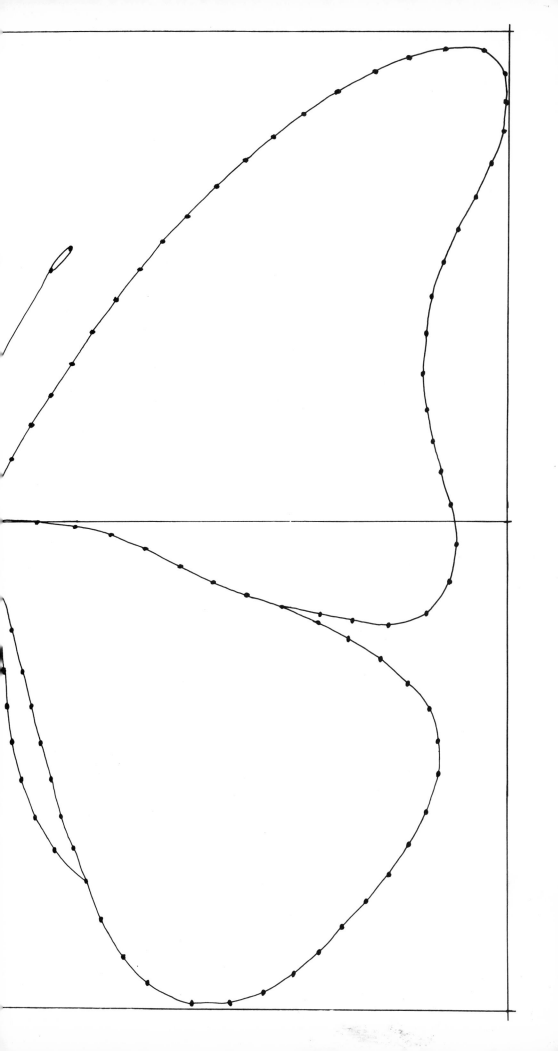

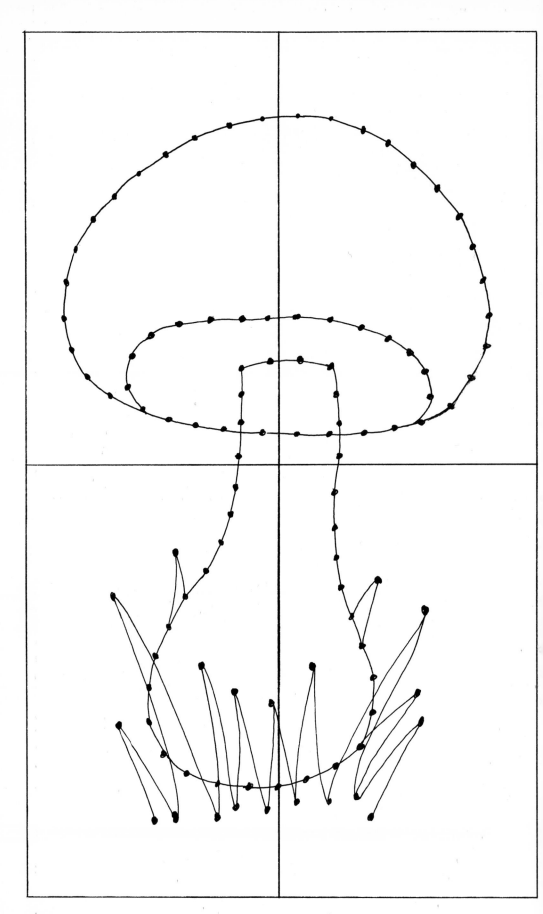

Mushroom pattern, nail markings placed by personal judgment

Transferring a Circle Pattern, Pounding Nails, and Stringing

Once the picture is drawn on paper and clearly marked as to placement of nails, I tape (with masking tape) the paper to the wood. I then drill, using a 1/16" drill bit or smaller, fairly shallow holes into the wood through each marking on the pattern. I then remove tape and pattern and can easily pound nails into marked holes. The nails should be pounded deep enough to feel very secure since the pull of yarns applies quite a bit of pressure. Unless a different effect is being sought, I try to pound the nails as evenly as possible so that the picture itself and not the nails is what attracts the eye. I have found it helpful to have tweezers on hand when pounding nails to hold the nails when there are many close together or in places that make them hard to hold by hand.

The pattern or design can also be transferred by pounding nails through the pattern into the wood, but it probably takes as much time to tear the pattern away as it does to do the drilling; there is also the disadvantage of a torn and probably not reusable pattern as well as the difficulty of making sure the paper is completely removed from around the nails. I recommend this method of transferring the pattern if one does not have access to a drill, if one has no desire to save the pattern, and as a way for this art form to be used by young people, as in the classroom.

I suggest that for your first symmograph you begin with a circle. This will give you a feel for the art of symmography and an understanding of its most basic concepts.

Prepare the wood as directed earlier. Then cut a piece of paper the size of your wood. Mark the center and with compass point at center, draw a circle of desired size. Mark points for nails evenly spaced around the perimeter. An even or odd number of nails can be left to your discretion. Possibly the easiest way to divide a circle evenly is to place a protractor along a diameter of the circle and centered in the middle of the circle. Mark off by degrees (five, ten, or whatever) around the outside of the protractor, as shown in top photograph. Then

Use of protractor to determine nail placement

lay a ruler so that it lines up with the center of the circle and the marks from the protractor and intersecting the outer circle you have drawn with the compass. Mark where it intersects the circle for nail placement, as shown in bottom photograph.

Transfer your pattern and pound your nails as evenly as possible. I have illustrated here transferring the pattern by drilling and then pounding as well as the alternate method of pounding the nails through the pattern into the wood.

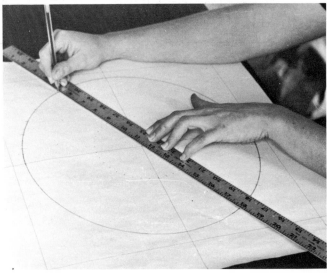

Marking nail placement

Transferring nail placement, using electric drill

Pounding nails

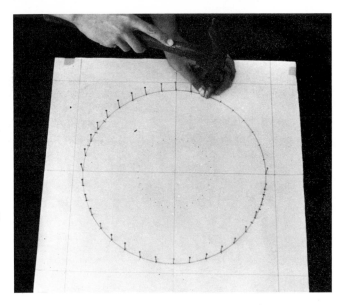

Transferring pattern and
pounding nails as
one step

Choose your yarn colors and begin by tying on the yarn
that you want to be at the center of the circle.

Tie on first color
and begin Basic Weave

17

Draw yarn directly across the circle, around the nail, back and around the nail next to the beginning nail. Work around circle using the Basic Weave either once or twice around. Tape end on back side of board to allow for changing your mind.

Beginning of second color of circle

Tie second color onto a different nail from the first (so as not to make any one nail's load too bulky) and draw yarn about a third of the way around circle, around nail and back around neighboring nail to start of this color.

Third color of circle

End of third color of circle

Continue to fill out circle using the Basic Weave and colors as desired. The final color to complete the circle should be done with the Edging Weave, either inside or outside the circle. If pleased with the results you can tie knots and weave ends in to finish.

Filling out circle

Example of circle

Stringing "The Bridge"

The first step is choosing the yarns to be used in this project and specifically which color will go where. This is sometimes a lot harder than it sounds since the colors combined as they are in the picture and in combination with the background very often produce an effect different from the artist's conception. Trial and error is the only method I can recommend. Eventually you begin to anticipate some of the possible results, but even after a great deal of experience, I am often fooled. I can only encourage the pursuit of the struggle until you are indeed satisfied. This frequently involves taking off the yarn and redoing it, but it is worth it.

A second important consideration is to realize the picture's three-dimensional quality. By this I mean you should ask yourself the following: What area of the picture recedes the most and therefore must be done first? What areas are in the foreground? What must overlap what to obtain the perspective desired? I found that it is often helpful to number on the pattern the areas in their "perspective order" so I can easily refer to it and do not end up having to undo and restring unnecessarily. The need for this consideration of the perspective order is obvious in The Bridge shown here in that the far side of the bridge that must definitely be done first, then the main supports,

The Bridge. Exemplifi
need to consider
"perspective order"

and then the side closest to the observer. However, in even the most basic symmographs, you must provide for a wing to overlap a body or a petal to overlap a stem.

I have illustrated here a step-by-step stringing of The Bridge to enable you to get a better idea of the actual process. I should explain that in this case, because the bridge extends all the way to the edges of the wood, I have pounded nails into the sides of the wood for attaching yarn and to string around when necessary. The first yarn is attached to one of these nails on the upper right-hand side where the cables of the bridge go off the picture. The nails are pounded in so that about 1/4" remains extended, and when the picture is completely strung, I pound in the nails on the edge and they are covered by the frame.

An alternate possibility for a situation like this is to put a tack on the back of the picture to hold the yarns that need to go off the edge. There are not, however, very many instances in which this situation will arise.

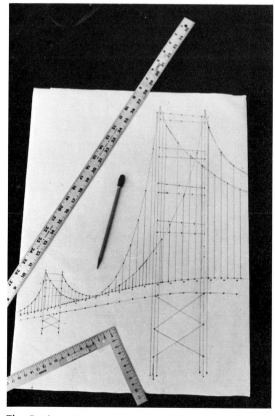

The Bridge. Pattern

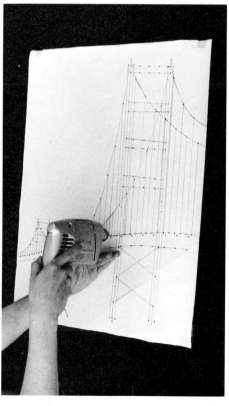

The Bridge. Transferring pattern

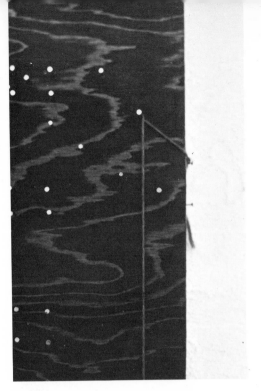

The Bridge. Tying first yarn onto nail on side of picture

The Bridge. Beginning to string picture

The Bridge. First color yarn (goldish-brown) completed

The Bridge. Beginning second color (orange)

The Bridge. Continuing stringing in
"perspective order"

The Bridge. Continuing stringing in
"perspective order"

The Bridge. Completely strung

The Bridge. Continuing stringing in
"perspective order"

Other Methods of Stringing

I usually string a picture while sitting on the floor. I find that being above my work is less tiring for the winding process and prevents some of the tangling of the yarn around the nails, though this does happen anyway.

Once you are aware of the "perspective order" you are ready to begin. Tie the first color with a square knot onto a nail, leaving a 3"–5" end for weaving in later. Try to place this knot where it will be later unnoticeable if possible (where the weave of yarns will later cover) but avoid overloading a nail that will be carrying a heavy burden. (What I mean by a heavy burden is a nail that must be used over and over to complete the design.)

For the most part, the actual stringing of the picture is a winding back and forth, returning each time to a different nail, either the next one or skipping one. I will refer to this as the Basic Weave or Basic Winding Method. This can be clearly seen in Diagram 2, and the Daisy illustrates what can result from the use of the Basic Weave.

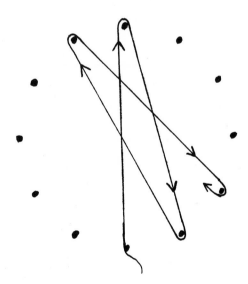

Diagram 2. Basic Weave

I found that the best way to learn what will happen is to experiment and see for myself. There are numerous possibilities. I will illustrate and describe here some of the basic concepts and hope that you will take off from there.

Daisy. Each petal and center done in Basic Weave

Filled and Hollow Circles: I distinguish between two different kinds of circles. One I call a Filled Circle, the other a Hollow Circle. The Filled Circle offers the possibility of the whole area of a circle of any size being covered by the woven yarns. The Hollow Circle contains within it a circle through which the background will show. The deciding factor as to which circle you will obtain is one nail. A Filled Circle is created by having an even number of nails, and a Hollow Circle is created by having an odd number of nails.

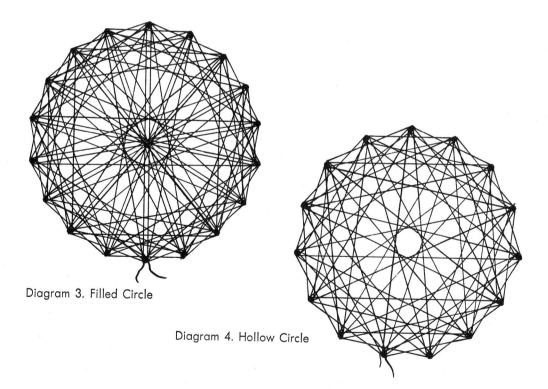

Diagram 3. Filled Circle

Diagram 4. Hollow Circle

A Filled Circle can also be made hollow by not stringing yarns directly across the circle, but a Hollow Circle (with an uneven number of nails) cannot be filled in by using the Basic Weave. The reason the Hollow Circle cannot be filled in is that, due to an uneven number of nails, there is no nail directly across the diameter of the circle from any other nail and therefore no way to cross the circle to fill in the center. See Diagram 6.

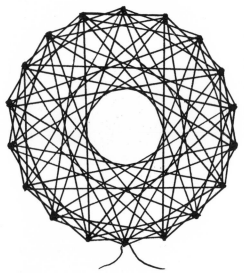

Diagram 5. Filled Circle left hollow

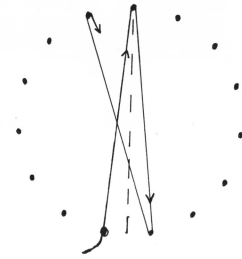

Diagram 6. Hollow Circle cannot be filled in center

To see how these concepts might be utilized within a picture we might compare the eyes of the Owl (Filled Circle), the Parrot (Hollow Circle), and the Frog (Filled Circle left hollow).

Frog. Eyes are Filled Circles left hollow to let wood show through

Owl. Eyes exemplify Filled Circles

Parrot. Eye uses Hollow Circle principle

So far I have been discussing filling or not filling circles by stringing the first yarn across the center of the circle and working the successive colors out toward the edges to fill it out.

Beginning of circle worked from center out

Another way to make a circle is by starting at the edges and working in toward the center as I have done in the Green Circle illustrated here.

Green Circle.
Worked from edges to center

This technique gives a slightly different effect. Your first yarn is tied on and you actually begin with an edging weave.

Beginning to fill circle starting at the edge

Beginning of second layer

Each time around the circle you are crossing more toward the middle of the circle until your final layer does cross the diameter (or the closest nail to it as in a Hollow Circle).

Star: The Star effect is really an incompletely filled circle. It is created by the Basic Winding Method, beginning by crossing the diameter of the circle and winding back to a neighboring nail or skipping one or more. The chubbiness of the Star's points depends upon how many nails are skipped in the winding process or how far apart the nails are.

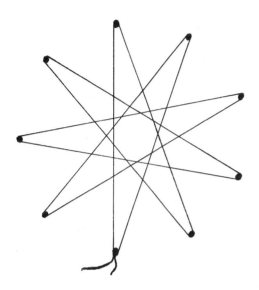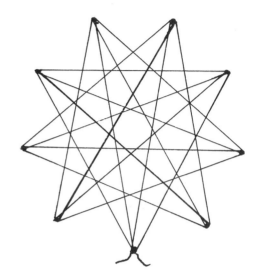

Diagrams 7 and 8. Stars
The Star is an effective technique in many designs.

sign I. Star

Design II. Star

Edging: The technique called Edging is used in filling out a circle, but is also put to use whenever a smoothly woven line (usually a curved line) is desired. This can best be shown by the diagram below.

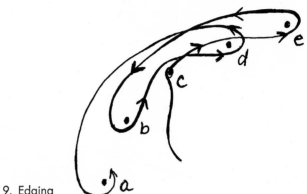

Diagram 9. Edging

The Edging is done by starting at a nail labeled **c**. Pass by nail **d**, loop around nail **e** and back around nail **b**, bypass nail **c**, go around nail **d** and back around **a**, etc. The direction in which one goes around the nails varies the effect produced. The Edging Weave can be done either inside or outside the curved line (see Diagram 10).

The Edging technique is probably one of the easiest and most widely used. It can be used as merely a border or outliner as in the butterfly shown here or it can be an essential part of the picture itself as in the Red and Orange Flowers.

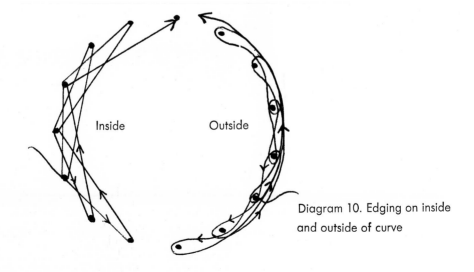

Inside   Outside

Diagram 10. Edging on inside and outside of curve

Butterfly I. Edging used as outliner

Orange and Yellow Flowers. Edging as an essential part of picture

Curve From Within and **Curve From Without:** Another concept which I consider extremely basic to the art of symmography is the ability to form a curved line by various straight lines either from without or from within the curve. This is probably most dramatically demonstrated by the picture shown here which has been entitled "Kite."

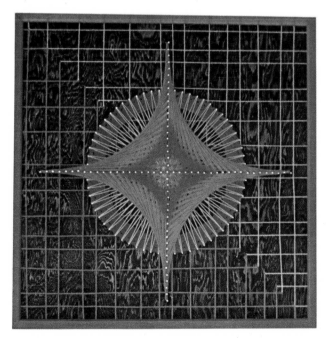

Kite. Curve from Without over Curve from Within

So far we have been mainly discussing the formation of curves by straight lines within, such as in the case of the circle.

Peace. Curve from Within

However, by drawing angles of varying degrees and using the Basic Weave, a curve can also be established from without. See diagrams below.

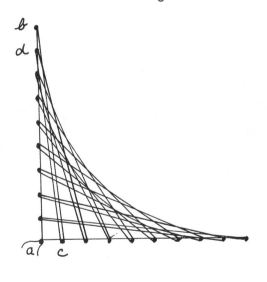

Diagram 11. Curve from without

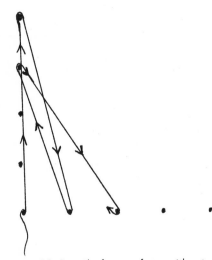

Diagram 12. Detail of curve from without

The smoothness of the curve here again depends upon the number and placement of the nails.

Filler: Still another "basic" that I must deal with is that of the Filler. The necessity of the Filler establishes itself predominantly in odd-shaped areas where one of the more ordered weaves is not possible. The Filler is not so much a weave as a back and forth winding of the yarn to cover space. This is illustrated in the leaf below and can be seen clearly in the head of the Dragon.

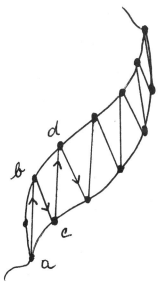

Diagram 13. Filler

Dragon. Filler

Leo. Filler in face and mane

The mane and much of the face of Leo pictured here illustrate the use of the Filler technique.

33

Wing Weave: Another technique I use often in symmography is what I have called the Wing Weave. This is exemplified by the wings of the Butterfly (page 52) and the Owl below. However, the concept can have a broader application and can be adopted when the need arises. Let's take a close look at the wing of the Owl.

The problem was to fill in the surface of the Owl's wing and border it with a second and third color but filling in more of the top part of the wing than the bottom, meanwhile retaining the symmetrical balance. This sounds overwhelmingly complicated, but it really is not. Let us look at it, one step at a time. In the diagrams below I will show only the step being explained to avoid too many confusing lines. Each diagram is accompanied by one or more illustrations to show the step as it might be in a picture.

In Step 1, the surface is covered by attaching yarn (gold) at point **a**. Point **b** is found by counting off and finding the nail which is numerically halfway around the wing (numerically, since it may not be obvious to the eye, such as in a butterfly wing). I then use the Basic Weave around once, without skipping any nails.

To fill in a little more completely, I can go around once more (Step 2).

Diagram 14. Wing Weave. Step 1

Wing Weave. Tying on first yarn.
Step 1

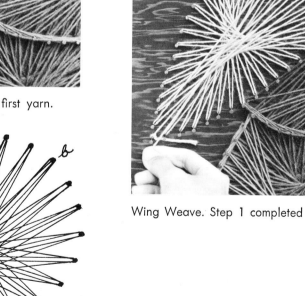

Wing Weave. Step 1 completed

Diagram 15. Wing Weave. Step 2

35

Wing Weave. Step 2

The second color (brown) of the Owl's wing (not always used in the Wing Weave) is attached at point **b**, drawn down around point **c** (which is about 2/3 of the way down the wing), back up around **d** and proceeding in the Basic Weave around to point **f**, even with **c**. See diagram.

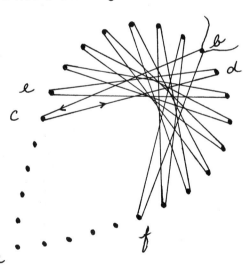

Diagram 16. Wing Weave. Step 3

This step (Step 3) can also be achieved by attaching the yarn about where **c** or **f** would be and wind the yarn up and around **b**, back around **h**, and continue in the Basic Weave. (see below).

Wing Weave. Ending Step 3

Wing Weave. Beginning Step 3

The addition of a third color (orange) of the Owl's wing (Steps 4 and 5) is really the principle I am trying to get across in the Wing Weave for its broader application. Tie on yarn at **a**, draw yarn partway up the wing to a point labeled **e** (distance up varies according to your discretion). Using the Basic Weave back around **g**, etc., continue to point **h** even with **e** on the other side.

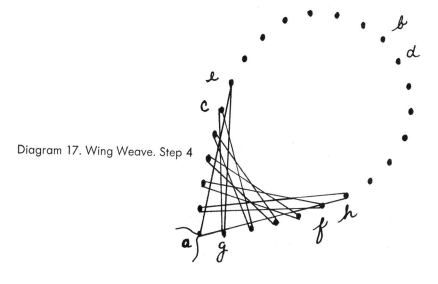

Diagram 17. Wing Weave. Step 4

Wing Weave. Beginning Step 4   Wing Weave. Ending Step 4

The next problem is to border the top half with a wider border and to attain a curved appearance on the inside as well as the outside edge. To get a slight border at the wing's sides, cross back down to point **i** to begin filling in the upper wing. I chose point **j** to begin the Basic Weave around the top half of the wing. Point **j** varies according to the amount you desire filled in. If point **j** is moved farther around toward **e**, more of the center of the wing will be filled in. If it is placed closer to **h**, there would be only a thin border produced. Then continue with the Basic Weave until the strand of yarn is directly across from the start of this step, point **k**.

Diagram 18. Wing Weave. Step 5

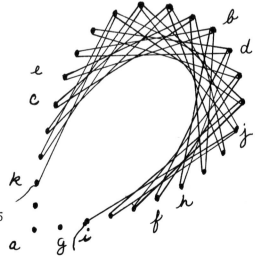

Wing Weave. Beginning Step 5

Wing Weave. Ending Step 5

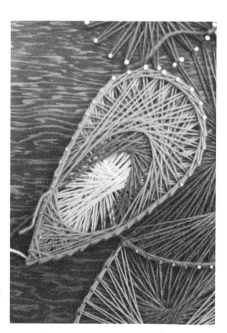

Wing Weave. Step 6, Edging

The final layer of the wing is done in the Edging Weave to ensure a smooth-looking edge and to outline. To obtain a more feathery look, this can be foregone.

Finishing

The matter of finishing can be a very deciding factor in the quality of a symmographic effect. As each color yarn is finished or each section of each color, I tape the strand to the back of the wood before cutting it off, since I very often change my mind as to what colors or what arrangement I want, and this way the strand can be reused. Once in a while I see something I would like to change by adding a color but find it should have been added many layers sooner. Instead of taking the whole picture apart and undoing the sections I do like, I thread a needle with the color yarn desired and repair the picture by weaving the color in under as many layers as necessary. This is tedious but sometimes worth the effort.

When I do achieve the desired effect, I cut and tie the finishing end around the nail where it ends. If it ends where it began, I also tie the beginning and ending strings in a square knot. I then thread a plastic yarn needle with one (or both) of the ends. (The advantage of a plastic needle is that it can bend around nails when necessary.) I then draw the end under the design so it will not be conspicuous from the front view (See Illustration below).

Finishing. Threading yarn under design.

Sometimes tweezers are needed to pull the needle through the design. When a few inches of the loose end are hidden from view, clip the remaining end. Repeat this procedure until all ends are hidden and cut.

Interesting Variations

The possibilities for variations in symmography are numerous. One way to achieve a different effect is to use different size nails in the same picture, as I have done in Kite (shown on page 31). This can increase the three-dimensional effect and allow for more perspective. In the case of the Owl (shown on pages 27 and 34), the nails of the eyes are longer than the rest to allow for the many layers of yarn.

Another variation may be seen in Mandala. Here I have used the inside ring of a small quilting hoop, drilled and pounded nails, and incorporated the ring into the design. It offers a second surface level. The only thing holding the hoop onto the picture is the even tension of the orange and yellow visible strings.

Mandala. Inside ring
of quilting hoop
provides second surface level

The quilting hoop can also form the structure of the picture itself. This is exemplified by Happy Strings and in the free hanging as well as the mounted hoop pictured below. Cup hooks and brass linoleum tacks have been used instead of nails and produce slightly different effects.

Another possibility is to drill holes all the way through the background wood and thread yarn through to form one layer of the picture. The Spider shown here is a good example of this, in that the web was spun flat to the wood and the spider

Happy Strings. Quilting hoop with cup hooks

Free hanging hoop with brass linoleum tacks

Mounted hoop with cup hooks

woven on top of it. By this I mean that, for the web, I have drilled clear through the wood and have threaded the yarn through with a yarn needle. In this way it is much like needle-work. The long supports of the web were done first and the spiral starting at the center and working out to the edge was done next, holding the long rays in place. The spider itself is done with nails as a regular symmograph. I have shown the back of the picture here to illustrate how the web goes all the way through the wood.

Spider. Yarn threaded through wood

Back of Spider symmograph

Still another variation is the possibility of covering the wood with a piece of material instead of staining or painting. In the Yin Yang pictured here, the black and white Paisley fabric is glued to the background wood. The nails for the design are then pounded through the fabric into the wood and strung with yarn.

Yin Yang. Cloth on wood as background

Rooster. Con-Tact paper
on wood as background

Con-Tact paper is another possibility along this line. In the Rooster pictured here the background wood has been covered with Con-Tact paper and then the normal procedure of transferring the pattern, pounding nails, and stringing the pictured was followed.

In cases such as the Rooster and the Yin Yang, because the background is so decorative, the design itself must remain extremely simple.

You might also produce a different effect by using two different colors of yarn as though they were one in stringing the picture. I have done this in the Rainbow of Bubbles pictured here, and the Green Circle (pictured on page 28).

44

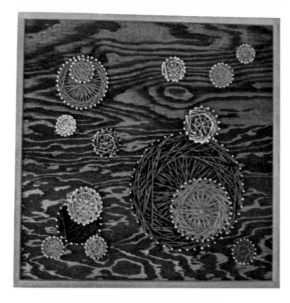

A Rainbow of Bubbles.
Two strands wound as one

Each "bubble" is made by the use of the Basic Weave to create a filled circle. Looking closely at the individual circle, there are two colors of yarn in each circle. For instance, one is light and dark blue, one is orange and rust, and the largest is navy blue and red. Instead of using one strand of four-ply yarn when doing the Basic Weave, I have used two strands as though they were one. Here is a close-up of a few of the "bubbles" to enable you to see this technique more clearly.

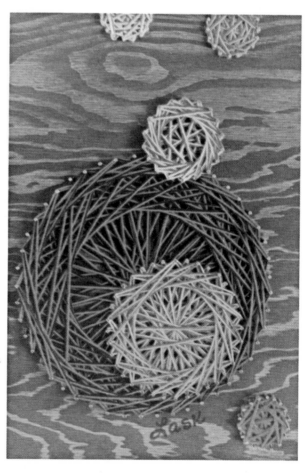

Close-up of A Rainbow of Bubbles

Another way to produce this kind of a "tweedy" effect might be by separating two of the four-ply strand of two colors of yarn and combining them to use as one strand. The variegated colored yarns produce still another effect, as can be seen here.

Variegated Star

The possibilities seem endless. Here, for instance, I took three scraps of wood to use as my working surface. The background wood is just an odd-shaped piece that I found. The two circles were left from a beanbag board we made for our son. I figured out how I wanted to use the three surfaces in a design, made one large pattern and also a small pattern with

Odd-shaped pieces of wood used for symmograph

nail placement for each circle, stained each surface, and transferred nail markings. I then pounded all the nails and strung the picture. The two small circles are held into place on the background wood by the tension produced by the green yarns shown in the picture.

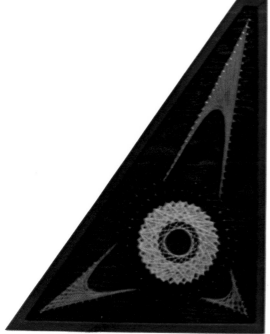

Centering

The red and blue design below illustrates still another possibility. The center design is done on a small square piece of pegboard (4 holes × 4 holes) that has been painted blue to match the background. I drilled one additional hole in the center of the pegboard square because I wanted all the yarns threaded through there. With a yarn needle and strand of red yarn, I threaded the pegboard to get the design I wanted. The ends were tied at the back of the pegboard. I then transferred the pattern for the nails onto the background wood. The pattern had the size of pegboard figured into it so there would be room left for correct placement. At the four corners of the pegboard I had separators which hold the pegboard out from the background wood.

These are small cylinders that can be bought at hardware stores. I painted them blue so they would not show. To hold the pegboard in place and also as part of the design I put a nail through each of the holes of the pegboard's perimeter. When all the nails were pounded (in this picture I used 1-1/4" nails), all that was left was to string the remainder of the picture, which is basically Curves from Without.

Pegboard Star

If one has any knowledge of needlework it is possible to combine some of these skills in making symmographs. As an example, the Giraffe shown here has a mane and tail that are made by adding fringe to crocheted chain stitching. The loops of the chain are then placed over the nails and the body of the giraffe is strung over them.

Needless to say, the field of symmography is wide open, waiting to be explored. To me, one of the greatest things about this art form is that I felt successful, from the beginning,

Giraffe. Fringed mane and tail

48

with a simple circular design. Since even the very simplest effort can prove pleasing to the eye, this technique can be experimented with by people of all age levels, from the grade-schooler, who can pound nails either with or without a pattern and string yarn between them, to the accomplished artist.

Additional Illustrations

Raggedy Ann

Raggedy Andy

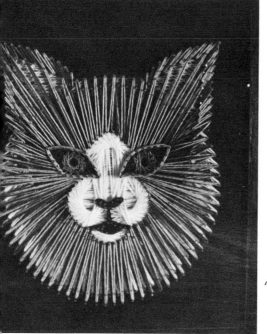

"Fat Face"

Roadrunner

Hummingbird with Flowers

Luna

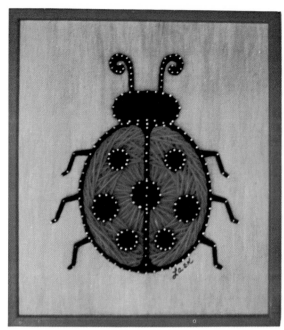

Ladybug

Large Quilting Hoop

Orange Toadstool

Butterfly II

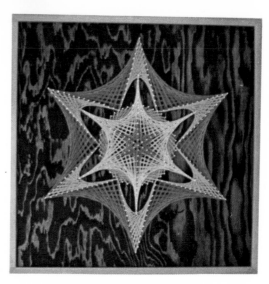

Orange Aestheometric

Panda

Red, White, and Blue

Black and White

Green-Yellow Star

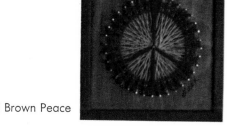

Yellow and Brown Peace

53

Fish

Yellow Flower

Three Stars

La Comédie

54

Red-Orange Flower

Orange Star

Red, White, and Blue Peace

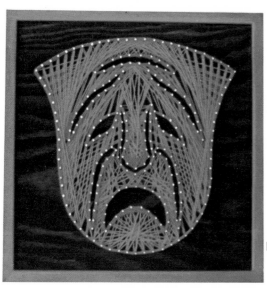

La Tragédie

A Word About Framing

When I first considered the possibility of selling my creations, I was fortunate in being directed to a most helpful woman named June Lederman, a San Anselmo, California, artist. One of her first suggestions was to take them home and frame them. Up until that point, I had never considered getting into framing, but with her encouragement and very simple instructions I embarked upon a whole new project. I found it very rewarding and just what my symmographs needed. I have kept my frames very simple and have done all my framing with a few basic, inexpensive tools. Since the frames really do a lot to finish the symmographs, and the process is not difficult, I will describe the procedure.

Framing—Materials Needed

Miter Box and **Miter Saw:** The miter box and saw are used for cutting accurate angles. Miter boxes range in price from $2 to $150. I settled on the $19 variety and find it adequate.

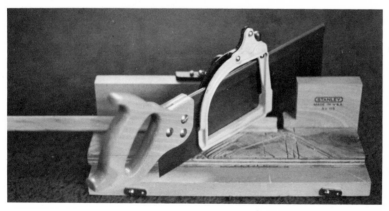

Miter box, saw, and molding

Molding: These are the strips of wood which are used for the frames. They can be purchased at an art supply store or lumberyard. If you can find what you want at a lumberyard, it is much cheaper. I began by using a very simple outside corner and shelf cleat or shelf bracket. I have not found much of a selection in the low price range since the pictures are quite thick and need a deep side to cover them. I have tried the straight strip of molding, but I do not prefer it since it

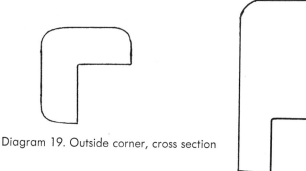

Diagram 19. Outside corner, cross section

Diagram 20. Shelf cleat or shelf bracket, cross section

Corner clamp

is extremely difficult to get it cut to fit perfectly; also, if you do your own cutting, you may not have four perfectly cut edges. For the most part I use the outside corner. In Diagrams 18 and 19 you can see a cross section of the outside corner and shelf bracket to help you to know what to look for.

Corner Clamps: These are for gluing and holding corners in place. Four are needed for most pictures.

Glue: A white, hard, and clear-drying glue is needed for gluing corners.

Brads: These are headless nails, used to secure corners. I like 1/2″ to 3/4″ lengths.

Punch: This is a metal tool that is used for setting nails. It can usually be found in a set of drill bits or can be bought separately at a hardware store.

Silicone Spray: This is useful in keeping the saw from sticking.

Hammer

Nail Hole Filler: I use plastic wood that comes in a tube or putty that comes in a stick.

Paints: I prefer acrylics.

Push Points: These are for securing the picture to the frame.

Braided Wire and **Screw Eyes** or **Sawtooth Picture Hangers:** These are necessary for hanging the finished product.

Framing–Procedure

To begin a frame, after measuring the picture, cut four pieces of molding with 45° angles to fit around picture.

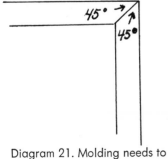

Diagram 21. Molding needs to be cut at 45° angles

Molding cut for frame

Place pieces in gluing clamps to hold at a 90° angle. Glue and tighten clamps. Leave several hours (overnight is best).

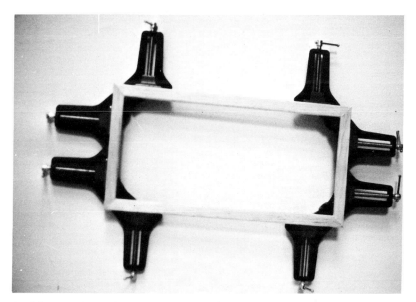

Molding in gluing clamps

When dry, drill two (or more, if needed) tiny holes (1/16" drill bit or smaller) at each corner and put in brads. I like 5/8", 3/4", or 1" brads, depending on the size and thickness of the frame.

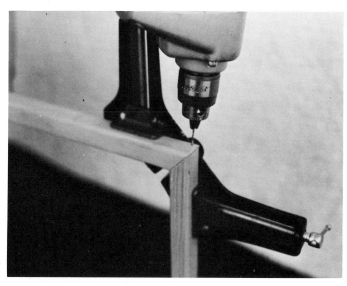

Drilling holes for brads

Set the nails with drill set or punch. To set a nail means to pound it below the surface by pounding a long punchlike tool which rests on the brad. A couple of light taps drives the brad below the surface of the wood.

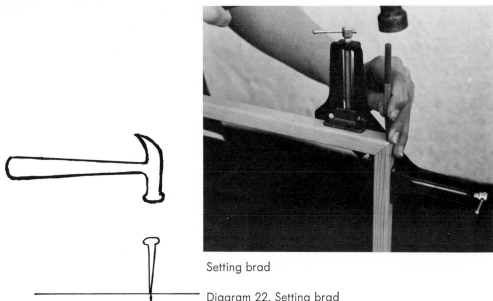

Setting brad

Diagram 22. Setting brad

Fill the nail holes with plastic wood. Fill generously since plastic wood can be sanded down and it does shrink in drying. Sand and stain or paint the frame, applying as many coats as necessary to get desired shade.

Place picture in the frame. The picture can be held to the frame in various ways. One way is by drilling and nailing 3/4", 1", or 1-1/4" brads through the sides of the frame and picture, filling the holes, and repainting. Some other possibilities are a screw and screw eye combination or a mirror holder and screw. The best way that I have found, however, is using push points that can be found at most hardware stores. With a screwdriver, the point is pushed into the side of the frame and there remains an extension of metal to hold the picture in place (see diagram and illustration below).

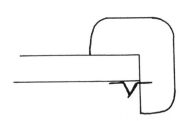

Diagram 23. Cross-sectional of push point holding picture to frame

Securing push point to frame

Spraying and Cleaning

I have sprayed symmographs with Scotchgard as a protector. The symmographs can be cleaned by blowing the dust off or vacuuming lightly.

Hanging the Symmograph

All that is left now is to equip the symmograph with what is needed to hang it. There are two good possibilities. One is to drill and screw in small screw eyes, either on the frame or very close to the edges of the picture. Using a braided wire, wrap it around the screw eyes twice and finish by wrapping it around itself several times. Do this at each side.

The other method is to screw on sawtooth picture hangers at the two upper corners. These are sold at most hardware stores or art supply stores. Many people find these preferable in that, once hung successfully, the picture does not tip.

Back of finished picture, ready to hang with screw eyes and braided wire.

Index